The **Four Seasons**

Beyond Autumn Leaves on the Other Side of the Moon

Anthony Di Micco

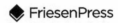

FriesenPress

Suite 300 - 990 Fort St
Victoria, BC, V8V 3K2
Canada

www.friesenpress.com

Illustrations by Dewitt Studios

ISBN
978-1-5255-8362-9 (Hardcover)
978-1-5255-8361-2 (Paperback)
978-1-5255-8363-6 (eBook)

1. POETRY

Distributed to the trade by The Ingram Book Company

To

my brother Martin,
my parents, Teresa Carlozzi and Giuseppe Di Micco,
and Anna who holds my hand.

SPRING

SUMMER

AUTUMN

WINTER

Preface

As with my first book, *Expressions of the Heart*, I invite the reader to experience what my heart has to say.

A good poem connects the heart of the poet to that of the reader. In so doing, it establishes a communion of two souls by becoming a venue of emotional and spiritual intimacy.

My heart has loved and been hurt, has had dreams and regrets, and has aspired to find God and the meaning of life. Its every heartbeat is a poem.

This book is divided into four sections or seasons, depicting four loose categories of poetry. Spring contains a short collection of childhood memories and children's poetry; summer, some love poetry; autumn holds largely contemplative poetry; and winter contains serious and thought-provoking poetry.

Anthony Di Micco

⤳ **Spring** ⤳

A Rainy Night Lullaby
(Lea's Lullaby)

Oh, my little one,
be not afraid.
Lie cradled in my arms,
for the rain is falling,
the wind is calling,
and the trees are dancing tonight.

Beyond the clouds, a rainbow's waiting.
Beside you, an angel prays.
In my heart, there is a song,
and the song is of you.

Oh, my little one,
don't you cry.
Close your eyes
and sleep,
for the rain is falling,
the wind is calling,
and the trees are dancing tonight.

A Happy Poem

I could write a happy poem,

if only you would
smile
at
me

and sing
The Wheels on the Bus
for me

and maybe
watch
a cartoon
with
me.

Peppa Pig
would be very nice!

ANTHONY DI MICCO

Tick Tock

Tick tock, eight o'clock;
time to go to bed.

Tick tock, eight o'clock;
time to get out of bed.

Mary, Mary

Where are you going, Mary, Mary?

I'm going to the deep blue sea.

And why are you going there, Mary, Mary?

To catch the big white fish.

And what will you do with the big white fish?

Bring him home to Mother.

And what will Mother say?

We'll just have to wait and see.

Ice Cream

I love ice cream with my eyes.
I love ice cream with my nose.
I love ice cream with my hands.
I love ice cream with my ears,
but most of all,
I love ice cream with my mouth!

Yum! Yum! Yum!

Thundering Little Horse

Thundering little horse
upon a golden hill.

You neigh, neigh, neigh!
Galloping, galloping, galloping!

I love you with all the clouds
and all the winds that blow.

Each morning, upon your hilltop.
Each night, inside my heart!

Angel

An angel holds the Book of Life,

mystic pages of burning light.

In a distant world,

on ancient clouds, he reads

the story of our lives.

Skies

Sky of blue and sun
brings children to the park.

Sky of dark clouds
brings rain and umbrellas.

Sky of moon and stars
brings sweet dreams.

Sweet Sofia

Silent as a shadow,
shy as a mouse,
with a tiny smile!

Halloween Night

One wicked witch
on Halloween night
flew over the hunter's moon.

Screech! Scat! Shoo!

Two little goblins
on Halloween night
made sweet pumpkin pies.

Screech! Scat! Shoo!

Three black cats
on Halloween night
walked on the garden fence.

Screech! Scat! Shoo!

Four wandering ghosts
on Halloween night
came knocking on my door.

Screech! Scat! Shoo!

Five scary mummies
on Halloween night
went for an evening walk.

ANTHONY DI MICCO

Screech! Scat! Shoo!

Six boys and girls
on Halloween night
said, *"Come outside and play!"*

Screech! Scat! Shoo!

Seven harvest mice
on Halloween night
held a party and danced.

Screech! Scat! Shoo!

Eight werewolves
on Halloween night
howled at the yellow moon.

Screech! Scat! Shoo!

Nine withered leaves
on Halloween night
ran away with the wind.

Screech! Scat! Shoo!

Ten trick-or-treaters
on Halloween night
went home to their warm, warm beds.

Screech! Scat! Shoo!

Three Baby Witches

Three baby witches
flew over the moon.
One was named Orange.
One was named Blue.
One was named Eva,
just like you!

The Balloon

The balloon man gave
me a red balloon.

My father painted it blue.

My mother painted it white.

I set it free of colours.

Honey on Bread

A

mother's prayer

is a shawl

over a child's soul,

and a mother's embrace

is honey on bread.

Days of the Week

On Monday,
I went to the zoo.
On Tuesday,
I went to the sea.
On Wednesday,
I went to pick cherries.
On Thursday,
I walked in the rain.
On Friday,
I went to the barber.
On Sunday,
I came back to you.

The Wind

This morning,
the wind blew my father's hat away.

This afternoon,
the wind chased after my mother.

Tonight,
the wind is quiet.

I think it must be sleeping.

To Ariana on Her Birthday

They say
that if you count
one hundred falling snowflakes
and make a wish,
your wish will come true.

One Christmas Eve,
five years or so ago,
a Christmas angel counted
one hundred and one falling snowflakes,
made a wish,
and you were born, making
the world
a little bit more beautiful!

Mirrors

Mirrors

are funny.

When Jenny looks

at her mirror,

she sees her twin sister!

The Sin

It was spring. The snow was melting
under the warm sun,
and my father and I had taken the bus
to the big city of Campobasso.

I found that the city took on
different sounds
and looks from my hometown.

The shoes, the clothes sparkled, and people
moved much more quickly,
shouting at what, I do not know.

And it was worst at the market.
The crowd reminded me of the ants back home,
crawling on sand hills, moving
every which way.

The smell of the city, too, was different.
My small town smelled of fruits and wind.
Campobasso smelled of brioche and ice cream
and petrol.

The stands at the market sold everything,
from women's purses to water bottles,
to balloons, to mortadella and bread.

We did quite a bit of shopping that afternoon,
and I was getting a little tired.

We finally came to a stand that sold toys:
funny toys, big toys, small toys, amazing toys!

By chance, I spied a green, wind-up toy frog.
I touched it.
The vendor looked at me and smiled.
My father had stopped to talk to a friend.
They talked for quite a while...enough time
for me to plan a robbery.

A fat lady came by to make a purchase
for her little girl.
While the vendor was distracted,
I bit my lips and took the step.
It was then that I grabbed the frog
and placed it in my pocket.
I quickly hid beside my father.

On our way home, on the bus,
I placed my hand over my pant's pocket,
covering up the sin hidden inside.
All the while thinking that
that toy was always mine.

Teeter-totter

You and I.
Teeter-totter!

I went up; you came down.
I came down; you went up.
Teeter-totter!

I talked; you listened.
I listened; you talked.
Teeter-totter!

I walked backward; you walked forward.
I bumped my head; you said, *"I told you so..."*
Teeter-totter!

~ **Summer** ~

The Butterfly

Motionless,

a butterfly hides in the meadows

among the hyacinths and the violets

till the sun comes up

and

kisses her

away!

Jenny's Song

Grey autumn days are on the roam.
The moon is on the rise,
and woe,
my one true love
is no longer by my side.

Fly, fly, my little song,
and tell Jenny
I remember
the golden days of summer,
running through the heather.

In a tree
a bird is singing,
nestled on a forest branch,
while the October winds are mourning
a long-lost summer love.

Fly, fly, my little song,
and tell Jenny
I remember
the golden days of summer,
running through the heather.

Twilight

A

time

when

sleep

fills

the

beating

heart.

Even When

Even when I can no longer kiss you
or love you...

even when my eyes are shut,
and you are not visible to me...

even when you are gone,
and I am lost in the mystery
of the eternal sleep...

I know
that a trace will linger,
a scent will stay,
and my soul will recall
the second, the minute, the hour of
your hand...

the first touch,
the first kiss,
the beginning...

of you!

Three Afghan Girls

I was watching
a documentary on RT television
the other night.

Three young Afghan girls
sat on sandy ground
in front of a black Kochi tent.
Their dark, nomad eyes were fixed
on an iPad that one of the girls was holding.

All three
lay covered
in loose, veiled clothing,
with only their hands and faces exposed
to the hot desert sun.

One of them
pointed to an image of a fashion model
on the computer screen.

She glanced at the other two
for only a brief, silent moment,
smiled, then turned her head
back to the computer
and remarked:

"She is as beautiful as a sapphire!"

I couldn't help but think
of three blue butterflies,
fluttering inside their cocoons.

If Love Is Not Possible

If you cannot be mine,

do not, at least, blind me

and deprive me of seeing you from afar.

Let me love you from a distance,

if only in my mind.

I will not kiss you;

I promise.

I will not touch your face;

I promise.

I will not stare into your eyes;

I promise.

I will not hold you tightly in my arms;

I promise.

Angie of 1932

Angie was kind,
and she looked like an angel.

She wore colourful dresses,
had pretty green eyes,
and wavy blonde hair.

She flirted jokingly
with every man she met.

She worked in a soup kitchen,
feeding the poor,
the old,
the ordinary,
and the lonely.

She was a living saint to all those
who believed
in the golden rule,
hard work,
purity,
God,
the family,
and
the American way.

(I heard she tragically passed away... in 1960 or so.)

ANTHONY DI MICCO

Love

My lips

touched yours

and then withdrew,

then came again

in time.

Breath of my breath,

inhaling life,

exhaling love!

First Kiss

The sun stained
the snow-covered forest
with a golden light
while frozen streams awoke
flowing silver through the meadows
where the flowers slept.
A linnet sang in rare delight,
as the sun came down
to render its gentle touch.
It was...
a small kiss upon a face
that rested pale, but beautiful,
in a winter's dream.

A Shakespearean Spring

When rain bursts forth from April clouds,
and flowers fill the meadows,
when a warmer sun fills the eastern sky,
and snow drips down from shingled roofs,
then Mary whistles a happy tune,
and her heart goes chasing after love!

When the robin hops in my backyard,
and my neighbour hangs her sheets to dry,
when the lilac tree begins to blush,
and the swallow builds his nest,
then Mary whistles a happy tune,
and her heart goes chasing after love!

Where Rivers Flow

There are two rivers

in my heart

that flow towards

two destinies.

One river flows

to your arms;

the other one flows

to an ocean,

where I drown.

Katherine of the Wind

Katherine, Katherine of the wind,
when will you love me?

You pull me into your arms,
and chain me to your whims.
You watch me beg, and you close your eyes.
You break my heart,
and I am left standing like a stone.

Katherine, Katherine of the wind,
when will you kiss me?

You hide there, behind the night,
where the wind blows wild,
and the stars cry out their songs.

Katherine, Katherine of the wind!
I am left standing here, like a stone.
When will you love me?

I Ran to You Without Words

I ran
to you, because
I loved
you without words.

When I first
saw you,
I could not speak.

Your beauty
stole all
the words hidden in my heart.

St. Claire

Cathedral jewel,

golden
mystical
stained-glass
angel,

sinless
heavenly
creature,

purple-veiled
in dress,

your
face
lily-white

your
eyes
sky-dipped blue,

your
head
crowned in purity.

Only
when the sun's in sail,
does your beauty
touch
my
eyes!

Lost Kisses

Old shoe boxes
hold many secrets—
sometimes even secrets of love.

I found an old photograph
of you the other day
between
two pages in a book.

I looked at it quietly—
nostalgically.

You were
much younger then,
with bright eyes.

You were
standing there
in a pink dress,
holding
a love poem that
I had written.

I saw you.
I saw the poem.
But not the kisses
I gave you.

Good Morning

The morning came
with toast and coffee,
a bowl of oranges, peanut butter, and jam.
The warm sunlight sat beside us
at the kitchen table.
And the cat on the balcony
wagged its tail, watching us.

"Good morning!"
We exchanged a smile or two.

"It's a wonderful day!"
I said.

"Want some Nutella?"
you asked.

"I love you!"
we said.

Your Lips

Your lips are like

a flower,

a bud,

so little,

so soft,

so red,

like a spring rose!

Uncertainty

I limped

going to see her.

I limped because

I was

only half

in love.

I bought two roses.

One, I gave to her.

The other rose,

was for my hesitation.

The Seagull

Above,
a seagull circles
the pristine blue sky,
white-winged,
outstretched,
lit in sunlight.

Below,
its shadow parallels
its movements
on the golden sand.

Summer Night

A
tiny
bird
is
perched
on
a
forest
branch.
Heart
beating,
watching
quietly,
patiently
waiting,
for
a
falling
star!

ANTHONY DI MICCO

Come to Me

Come to me
while the moon
lights the summer night,
and the jasmine tree
is sleeping.

While dreams
arrive on silver clouds,
scented in fingered winds.

While the old turret's clock
strikes the raven's wing,
and soft shadows roam the streets.

While lovers' hearts are aching,
and prayers of love are whispered.

Come to me!

Dark Clouds

A cold wind

is shooing me

away from

you.

I've become

a black bird on the horizon,

vanishing

into

eternity.

Claire

I've searched for you
by the fountain,
when the clouds of August
unveiled the moon,
and the stars flowered the sky.

The summer wind
brought the scent
of your perfume to me,
and the silence of the night
echoed your words of love.

At the darkest hour,
the fountain glistened,
and the image
of your face appeared.

For a while... a while...

until a teardrop fell,
and you were gone...

"Where were you, Claire?
You promised to love me!"

A Lazy Afternoon

The ocean
sighs.

(listen)

The waves dance
rhythmically
on the seashore.

(sleep)

The noonday sun caresses
our suntanned bodies.

(golden)

Lazily, I turn

to give you

a warm kiss.

(silence)

She

She walks softly
in the night.

(wind)

She smiles
and stares at the sky.

(kisses)

She spreads her arms
and points to me.

(fingers)

She calls,
and I am pulled into the stars!

(moon)

At the Beach

The sea yawns.

A gentle breeze straddles the clouds.

Falling asleep,

a little boy closes his eyes

as a dream washes ashore!

ANTHONY DI MICCO

I Will Miss You

I will miss you

when you are gone.

Your smile,

your voice in the long night,

your hand in my hand,

your gentle face,

the falling

leaves

of

poetry!

Madeline

You'd like to turn back the clock,
wouldn't you, Madeline?

But
the masquerade ball is done,
and the fireworks have all exploded.

It's way past the midnight hour,
and the crystal stars are gone.

Now,
only the night wind,
empty bottles,
and vacant chairs
are here
to welcome
you.

Did you think
that this was an unending,
summer night party?

The years have escaped us, Madeline.

The cold moon is laughing at you
and pities me.

Go away, Madeline.
The party's over.

Autumn

The Gifts of Autumn

Mellow gardens
brimmed
with
branches
of
golden fruit.

September skies
dripping
with
sunlight
over
amber fields
of
summer.

Never-ending days
of
soft
winds,
chrysanthemums,
and
afternoon
delights!

Tree Poem

A tiny branch
stretches to touch
the white moon,
begging
for
mercy.

Leaves falling...
leaves falling...

ANTHONY DI MICCO

The Wind

The wind chimes and caresses,
dances a pirouette,
blows out some candles,
and takes a bow!

Clap... clap... clap...
Bravo... bravo...

Why the Crying?

The trees around me are weeping!

Yes, they're shedding their sorrow
along with their falling leaves.

The days of summer have all run away,
and the mouth of a bitter winter
will soon open up
to swallow
all of autumn's
flesh.

But why now,
oh, trees of autumn,
are you weeping?

Don't you know that every death begins at birth?

Dry Leaves

Bent sky

over a crusted soul.

Peeled brown petals

running away

over hills of silence.

Winds

Railway tracks across the sky

on roads to the unknown.

A Reflection on Living

Walk in a cemetery.

Walk in a city.

Among the dead, all are dead.

Among the living, how many are alive?

Justice and Mercy

When
the
Messiah
comes,
Adolf
Hitler
will
weep
for
a
thousand
years,
and
a
Jew
will
comfort
him.

Speak

One should
speak.

Speak
with
the mouth.

Speak
with
the hands.

One should
speak
with
heart.

Speak
with
the
body
in a dance.

Truth can scream.

Kindness
can

be
a soft whisper.

Speak like a madman!

Speak like a saint!

But speak...

Speak... before it's too late.

Singularity

•

What Is Man?

What are bones and flesh
that they should carry
thoughts and dreams inside them?

That the hands of Man
should open up
like a flower,
and like a flower,
beauty then should emerge
to blossom and grow?

That his heart,
caged in dry ribs, cries out,
and armies form
to conquer
in love and war.

That the human eye,
using compass and square,
should measure the distant sky,
while anxious arms stretch out
to touch the quiet stars?

That Man's legs
move in time,
and in time,

ANTHONY DI MICCO

fall down to earth,
where the soul yields,
and life flies away?

1902

If the world were painted
in black and white,
would it be real?

Last night,
I watched a silent film,
circa 1902.

A grainy, flickering film,
full of trapped people
inside a celluloid world.

Men, women, and children,
hovering around a Kodak camera,
posing, gesturing, staring.

I smiled at them,
and they smiled back at me.
Voiceless people, laughing and waving.

Each of us in our own world.

If the world were painted
in many colours,
would it be real?

The Great Escape

She left me.
She wanted to run away from this world.
She had had enough of living
the plain life.
She said she wanted to escape—
escape all the ugliness of her reality.
So, she went to the museum,
looked at all the paintings
that hung
gold-framed and beautiful
on the walls,
and she said:

*"This one looks like a Renoir.
I like it!"*

And so,
she brush-stroked herself
into a field of flowers:
of purple lavenders,
red poppies,
and baby's breath.
Yes, she
brush-stroked herself into a masterpiece painting,
wearing a white dress,
a parasol,
and a smile!

On Sunday afternoons,
I sometimes
visit her
in her new world,
because I feel so sorry.

Traces

It is not what I am that continues,
but what I give existence to.

My immortality lies not in my eyes,
but in my tears.

Not in my failures, but in the seeds of my dreams.

I once stood at a train station.

When the train came,
I departed,
leaving nothing behind.

The Haves and the Have Nots

There are
those who have,
and those
who have not.

The Haves.

They sit
at a golden table,
drinking milk and honey.

The Have Nots.

They live
in an empty room.

Time

We

know

what

time

it

is,

but

do

we

know

what

time

is?

The Fable of the Spider and the Web

A spider was sitting
by a symmetrical sea
when a fly flew by
wanting to rest.

"Surely, it will be a wonderful thing
to lay my wings
on a sea of silver and wind!" said the fly.

The spider schemed...

"Come," said the spider.
"I will give you rest.
Enjoy the softness of my silver sea."

And so the fly,
assured and grateful,
embraced the web.

"Thank you, spider.
Your generosity
will not be forgotten," exclaimed the fly.

The spider
pounced upon her
and laughed.

They

Their eyes were made blind.

Their speech was censored.

Their ears were filled with lies.

Their mouths, poisoned.

Touching was prohibited.

And yet, they

continued to eat their grass

and graze contentedly in the field.

Gnostic Moon

Moon,
you come and go,
strewn among the fields of clouds.

The autumn wind rides
prancing, silently, across
the meadow of your scattered stars.

And you bend and rock
like a cradle, bearing night's
glowing lantern hung in time.

O Moon,
how bright your soul;
how much like the Sphinx you are!

You light humanity's way
through the dark night,
till the day breaks in a new world.

Winter

Evening Comes

The sun's

galloping in the sky,

leaving tracks of blood

behind.

Galloping, galloping,

the golden horse neighs!

Hoof after hoof,

breath after breath,

while the night horse

is in chase.

Crying

Crying

is

the

first

and

the

last

word

spoken

by

Man.

Beyond Autumn Days

Lost years fly over the sky

like migrating birds

when winter comes.

All beauty lies in memories,

and my past is more beautiful

than my present.

Mr. Smith

Mr. Smith would get angry.
His head would explode like a volcano.
He would look at the front doors of his condominium,
which needed repair.
Two little holes on the aluminum doors
irked him badly.

"Why are they not fixing them?
Damn administrators!
They are useless!
Maybe, I should plug them up myself!"

And then it happened.

He suffered a stroke last week.
He hasn't returned home; he won't ever return.
His mind, his body, is broken.
He wears diapers, mumbles to himself, and can't walk.

The doors are still where they were.
The holes are still there.

To
Mr. Smith,
they no longer are.

Boots

Dark brown leather.

Worn-out
old
boots.

No longer wanted.

Lying in my garage.

You served your purpose,
and now

cobwebs cover your scarred faces.

Look at yourself...

pathetic,

bruised,

stale...

Why are you still alive?

I put my feet inside you,
but you don't mind...

and neither do I.

The Funeral

Yesterday,
I observed
from my window
a coffin
with death inside.
Alleluia!

Mourners dressed in black
came with tears and white handkerchiefs
in their purses and pockets.
Alleluia!

Church bells
rang out, calling everyone to come and see.
Alleluia!

And afterwards, I observed, too,
that everyone went back to living their lives.
Alleluia!

They went back to their jobs.
They washed their handkerchiefs clean,
and they had pizza for supper.
Alleluia!

I Didn't

I didn't want to write a poem today, but

the words in my brain were barking like dogs
wanting to go for a walk.

I stood there,
pissed off.

Thinking:

*"Give me a break.
It's cold outside!"*

But I really love my dogs, so

I did.

Writing Poetry

I sometimes wander

lost

in clouds of words,

waiting for the lightning,

the thunder,

and the rain, to drop

upon empty pages.

Sometimes...

I wait for the tears.

Brotherhood

When
the
Messiah
comes,
the
gates
of
Paradise
will
be
opened
to
all
mankind,
and
Jacob
will
dance
naked
in
the
streets.

ANTHONY DI MICCO

When Snow Falls

They called her Queen Margret.

She was just a bag lady
who had walked the streets
of the city
for the last twenty or more years.

And now,
Queen Margret
lay abandoned,
mouth opened, ragged,
holding a tin cup
in her small, cold hand.

Beside her,
on a ripped cardboard sign,
she had written her will.

It read:

*"To the needy, I leave my tin cup,
to the naked, my rags,
to the homeless, the streets,
to the seasons, my memories,
to the unloved, my tears.
To the indifferent, I give you my life."*

Her body lay covered in snow,
against a wall,
for three days and three nights,
unnoticed,
while strangers walked by.

Saints

The snow came down
as a cold, white dust
over the churchyard.

I watched
while the frail priest shovelled
the snow
from the church steps.

He was old,
and had a reputation
of being
soft-spoken and kind.

In the churchyard,
a statue of a saint looked on
as he shovelled.

The snow continued to drop
covering
the statue
and the priest

until, we had two
saints
covered in snow.

My Winter Friends

The snow was white, boot-trodden,
and spotted with holes for playing marbles.
The air was cold, reddening our cheeks.

We wore woollen gloves that became wet with use.
The afternoon sunlight fell golden on the schoolyard,
as we flicked our marbles hoping to win a game.

It was always Mary, Peter, Giovanni, and me,
every day after school, playing marbles.

Wintertime brought us the sparkling snow,
but it also brought us its fun and the laughter.

Sometimes, we'd build a snowman
and had friendly snowball fights.
We played until the shadows
of the late afternoon sun touched our shoulders,
beckoning us to leave.

But Giovanni would always insist:

"Come on, Tony, one more game of marbles," he would say.

We were good friends,
and Giovanni was my best friend.

But that, was all, a long time ago...

The other day, I went back to the old schoolyard.
It was empty. Snow had fallen, covering the yard,
but not my memories.

An emptiness filled my heart when I learned
that our school had been converted
into an old folks' home.

The structure looked cold, cold like a tomb.
It had changed its skin. It had become grey,
and the windows were brushed in darkness.

As my eyes moved across its southern wall,
I saw a face; a face, looking down
from a window.

It was pale and hollow-cheeked, staring down at me.
I waved at it, but the face didn't wave back.

I paused for a moment,
lowered my eyes,
and... I sadly walked away.

I thought about the passing of time,
and the happy years of my childhood.

I thought about my winter friends,
and for one brief and painful moment,

I wondered...

I wondered, if that face at the window...
was Giovanni.

The Virus

A fog fills the night
while a cold drizzle of rain
keeps on falling on
the trembling trees,
and the shiny streets
that mirror the passing cars.

On television,
they're talking about a pandemic.

They're warning us about
a deadly virus.

They're telling us to be careful.

"Wash your hands,
check for cold symptoms,
take your temperature,
wear a mask,
keep your distance,

but please, don't panic;
you'll probably survive...

unless, you're old—
old enough to die."

Am I old enough to die?

I've seen the dark eyes of the wolf
that lives inside people,
and it scares me almost as much as
the virus.

But I'm thinking
that the world is good,
is alive
and kicking,

and that's all that it can do:

keep on breathing,

keep on loving,

keep on believing.

In the end,
I know we will survive.

The wind,
the rain,
the fog,
and the night
know it too.

ANTHONY DI MICCO

The Walkers

This morning
I saw the W a l k e r s.

Some w a l k i n g north.
Some w a l k i n g south.

Speechless
they walked under grey clouds.

Some w a l k i n g north.
Some w a l k i n g south.

Fearing the p l a g u e,
they quivered inside.

Some w a l k i n g north.
Some w a l k i n g south.

All wearing their m a s k s ... all going n o w h e r e.

Insomnia

The night
outside
is cold,
cold to the bone,
as the traffic lights
carry out their nightly routines
over the empty streets.

My eyelids
won't shut
even though
my mind
is spent.

I stand
alone
at my window
holding a glass of liquor
in my hand.

It's 4:05 a.m.

My heart and the night
are on an endless highway.

I feel my brain pounding,
full of self-inflicted wounds.

ANTHONY DI MICCO

I think about you.

I think about what I am,
and what I am not.

I search for meaning,
as a deep void settles in.

All the while...

I stand alone at my window,
watching the frozen world outside,
still sleeping.

My World

Where am I
in this pallid world
of despair?

This world
of blood-drained
streets and buildings.

This world
where the wind
runs through the sky,
leaving its cold breath
hanging on walls.

In the park,
the frozen trees
wave to me,
beckoning me to
save them.

But I am frozen, like them.

My summer is gone, like theirs.

And I can only recall
in solitude
the years
that have passed, and

ANTHONY DI MICCO

the dreams
that have withered.

I live in a world
where time is late,
and days are measured
in regrets.

Farewell

When I die,

I want to die

watching raindrops

tapping on my window,

waving goodbye!

Hell

I woke up

after I died,

and I found

myself on Earth.

I said to myself,

"This must be Hell!"

Cries from a Nursing Home

Mother,
who will give me bread?
Who will give me water?
Who will hold my hand, when
you are so far away?
Who will bury me,
after I die alone?

Drum

O Drum,
beating
in time
in a world of sorrow.

Run away!
Run away!

Abandon
my withered hands
and follow
the stream
of the years
where my dreams
echo
the innocence
of my childhood.

Go far away from me
and don't look back.

Only remember
that I was once that child
inside you,
beating.

The Vision

And I saw
a cold winter coming, bringing
wind and snow.

And I saw a child, waiting
by a warm ocean shore.

Waiting... waiting...

Beyond autumn leaves,
on the other side of the moon!

ANTHONY DI MICCO

When the Dark Night Ends

When the dark night ends,

the tree of love will
spread its branches
across the eternal sky
and the angel of pity
will stretch his ethereal wings
over our souls.

When the dark night ends,

the tears we shed
in the storms of night
will water our dreams
of salvation.

When the dark night ends,

repentance
will embrace forgiveness
and I shall embrace
you tenderly,
once more.

End

Lightning Source UK Ltd.
Milton Keynes UK
UKHW011834040621
384966UK00007B/738/J

9 781525 583629